STRAIGHT FORWARD

Math Series

BOOK 2

PRE-GEOMETRY

by S. Harold Collins

Book cover design by Kathy Kifer

Published by:
Garlic Press
605 Powers St.
Eugene, OR 97402

ISBN 0-931993-31-8
Order Number GP-031

www.garlicpress.com

To Parent, Teachers, and Students:

The Pre-Geometry Book 1 and Pre-Geometry Book 2 are part of our **Advanced Straight Forward Math Series**. They are designed for parents, teachers, and students.

These Pre-Geometry books will help parents and teachers direct students in the transition from basic mathematics to geometry. These two books are a natural extension of our Straight Forward Math series and Advanced Straight Forward Math Series which have presented the basic and advanced mathematical operations of addition, subtraction, multiplication, and division.

Pre-Geometry Book 1 and 2 provide the mathematical skills needed by students to succeed in geometry groupings. Abstractions and structured logic are kept to a minimum. Each pre-geometry topic includes an explanation and multiple exercises to reinforce the explanation presented.

Two measurement tools are provided. A Beginning Assessment Test will survey a student's beginning pre-geometry skill level. A Post Assessment Test will measure how well the pre-geometry skills have been mastered.

Exercises can be completed in the book or on separate paper. Answers to exercises are provided.

Contents

Beginning Assessment Test

1. Perimeter-Circumference. Match the geometric shape with the the formula.

___ 1. P = s + s +...+ s
___ 2. V = $\frac{1}{3}$ bh
___ 3. A = π r²
___ 4. A = l w
___ 5. C = π d
___ 6. P = 4s
___ 7. A = $\frac{1}{2}$ h(a+b)
___ 8. V = l w h
___ 9. A = b h
___ 10. P = 2 (l + w)
___ 11. A = $\frac{1}{2}$ b h

a. area of a rectangle
b. circumference of a circle
c. volume of a pyramid
d. perimeter of a polygon
e. area of a triangle
f. area of a circle
g. perimeter of a rectangle
h. area of a parallelogram
i. volume of a prism
j. perimeter of a square
k. area of a trapezoid

2. Find the perimeter or circumference of these figures.

a.

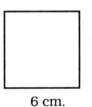

6 cm.

b.

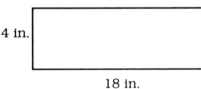

4 in.

18 in.

c. 3 m.

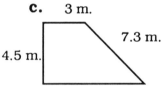

7.3 m.

4.5 m.

7 m.

d.

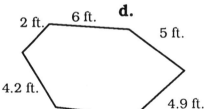

2 ft.   6 ft.

5 ft.

4.2 ft.

4.9 ft.

6 ft.

e.

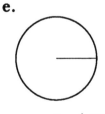

r = 4 cm.

f.

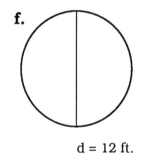

d = 12 ft.

3. Find the area of all the figures above except *d* .

4. Find the area of each figure.

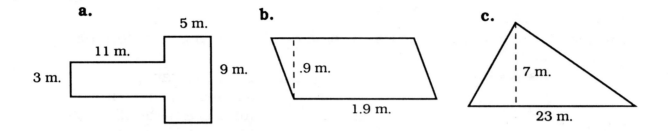

a.

5 m.

11 m.

3 m.

9 m.

b.

.9 m.

1.9 m.

c.

7 m.

23 m.

5. Find the surface area of this figure.

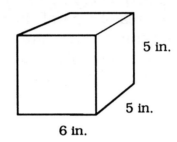

5 in.

5 in.

6 in.

6. Find the volume of each figure.

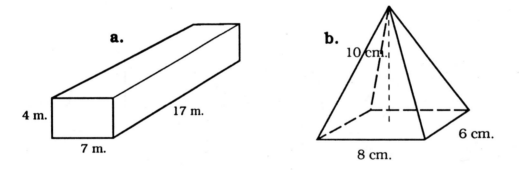

a.

4 m.

17 m.

7 m.

b.

10 cm.

6 cm.

8 cm.

Perimeter

Perimeter is the distance around a figure.

To find the perimeter (p) of a **polygon**, simply add together the length of all sides (s).

Use this formula: **p = s + s + ...+ s** .

For example:

5 in.   4 in.

4 in.   5.5 in.

7 in.

p = s + s + s + s + s

p = 4 in. + 5 in. + 4 in. + 5.5 in. + 7 in.
p = 25.5 in.

For **rectangles** and **squares** we can use special formulas to find perimeters.

Rectangles:

l = 10 in.

w = 4 in.

p = 2 (l + w)   l= length   w = width
p = 2 (4 in. + 10 in.)
p = 8 in. + 20 in.
p = 28 in.

Squares:

s = 3 in.

p = 4 s   s= side
p = 4 x 3 in.
p = 12 in.

Perimeter, Exercise 1. Use a formula to find the perimeter in each problem.

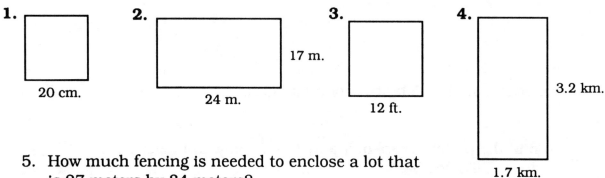

5. How much fencing is needed to enclose a lot that
    is 27 meters by 34 meters?
6. How much framing is needed to frame a 14 inch square picture?
7. The perimeter of a yard is 150 feet. Its width is 33 feet. What is its
    length?

Perimeter, Exercise 2. Find the perimeter of each figure.

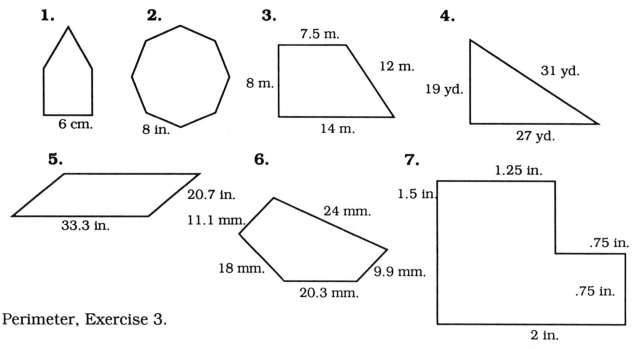

Perimeter, Exercise 3.

1. One side of an equilateral triangle is
   14.3 centimeters. What is the perimeter of the triangle?
2. Two sides of an isosceles triangle are 12 feet each. The perimeter of
   the triangle is 37 feet. What is the length of the third side?
3. One side of an equilateral triangle is 15 inches. One side of a square is
   10 inches. Which polygon has the greater perimeter? By how much?
4. A rectangle measures 24.7 meters in length and 104.4 meters in
   perimeter. What is the width?
5. A regular hexagon measures 72 yards in perimeter. What is the length
   of each side?

Circumference

Circumference is the distance around a circle.

Mathematicians have found that a relationship exists between the circumference and diameter of all circles. The circumference of a circle is slightly more than three times its diameter (actually 3.1415....). The number 3.1415... goes on forever. We have come to refer to this number as **pi**. It is represented by the Greek symbol π.

As a fraction, π is approximately $\frac{22}{7}$ or $3\frac{1}{7}$.

As a decimal, π is approximately 3.14.

This formula will give us the closest approximation of the circumference of a circle:

$$c = \pi d \qquad \text{circumference equals pi times diameter.}$$

Finding the circumference of a circle using fraction and decimal methods:

14 m.

d = 14 m.

$c = \pi d$
$c = 22/7 \times 14$ m.
$c = 308/7$
$c = 44$ m.

$c = \pi d$
$c = 3.14 \times 14$ m.
$c = 43.96$ m.

You can see how close each answer is. This is why we must say that the answers are close approximations.

Suppose you are to find the circumference of a circle. You know the formula is $c = \pi d$. But you have only been given the radius. You can still solve the problem. A diameter is equal to two radii.

Circumference, Exercise 1.

1. Find the circumference for each circle. Use 3.14 for π.

   a.

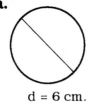

d = 6 cm.

   b.

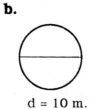

d = 10 m.

   c.

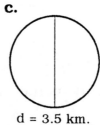

d = 3.5 km.

   d. Diameter:
      14 inches

2. Find the circumference for each circle. Use 3.14 for π.

   a.

2.5 in.

   b.

3.24 yd.

   c.

6 ft.

   d. Diameter:
      3.27 miles

   e. Radius:
      14 yards

3. Write a formula that will find the circumference for a circle when only the radius is given.

Area

Squares and Rectangles

Area is a number indicating the size of the inside of a plane geometic figure. Area is always measured in square units (i.e., sq. in.; or in.^{2}).

Rectangles

A rectangle is a quadrilateral with four right angles.

Area (A) of a rectangle equals length (l) times width (w).

3 cm.

A = l x w
A = 4 cm. x 3 cm.
A = 12 cm^2

4 cm.

Square

A square is a quadrilateral with four right angles and four sides the same length.

Area (A) of a square equals side (s) times side (s).

A = s^2
A = 4 km. x 4 km.
A = 16 km^2.

4 km.

Area, Rectangles/Squares, Exercise 1. Find the area using the correct formula.

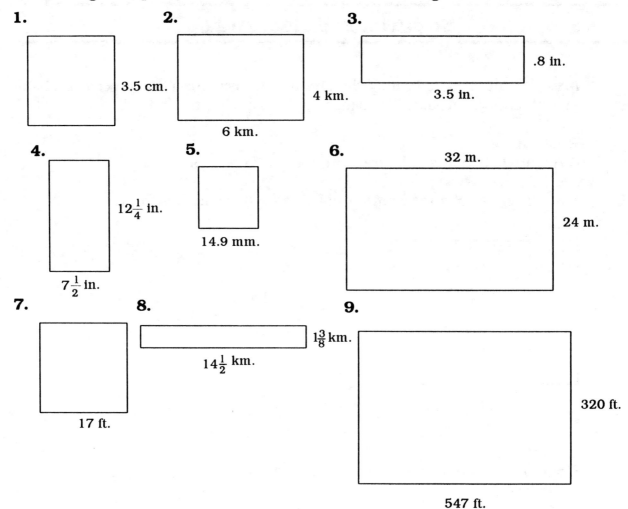

1.

3.5 cm.

2.

4 km.

6 km.

3.

.8 in.

3.5 in.

4.

$12\frac{1}{4}$ in.

$7\frac{1}{2}$ in.

5.

14.9 mm.

6.

32 m.

24 m.

7.

17 ft.

8.

$14\frac{1}{2}$ km.

$1\frac{3}{8}$ km.

9.

320 ft.

547 ft.

Area, Rectangles/Squares, Exercise 2.

1. How many 1 foot square tiles must be purchased to cover a 14 ft. by 11.5 ft. kitchen?

2. A large glass window which is 42 in. by 62 inches needs to be replaced. How many square inches of glass are needed?

3. How much paint is needed to cover a floor that is 8 meters by 10 meters? A quart of paint will cover 20 square meters. How many quarts must be bought to complete the job?

4. How many square yards in a 120 yd. by 50 yd. football field?

5. The area of a square is 196 cm.². What is the length of each side?

6. The area of a rectangle is 94.5 in.². The length is 9 inches. What is the width?

Area, Rectangles/Squares, Exercise 3. Find the area of each figure.

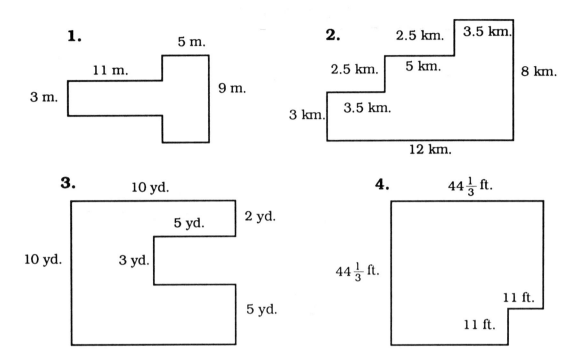

1.

5 m.

11 m.

3 m.

9 m.

2.

2.5 km.   3.5 km.

2.5 km.   5 km.

3 km.   3.5 km.

8 km.

12 km.

3.

10 yd.

5 yd.   2 yd.

10 yd.   3 yd.

5 yd.

4.

$44\frac{1}{3}$ ft.

$44\frac{1}{3}$ ft.

11 ft.

11 ft.

Area

Parallelograms

A **parallelogram** is a quadrilateral with two pairs of parallel sides.

The area (A) of a parallelogram equals base (b) times height (h).

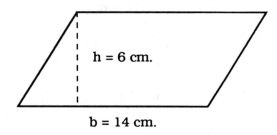

h = 6 cm.

b = 14 cm.

A = b x h
A = 6 cm. x 14 cm.
A = 84 cm.^{2}

Height is always perpendicular to the base.

Area, Parallelograms, Exercise 1. Use the formula to find the area of each parallelogram.

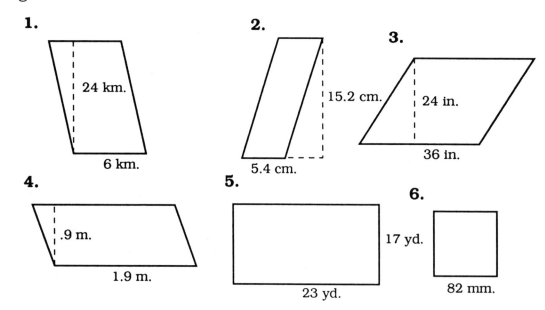

1.

24 km.

6 km.

2.

15.2 cm.

5.4 cm.

3.

24 in.

36 in.

4.

.9 m.

1.9 m.

5.

23 yd.

6.

17 yd.

82 mm.

7. b = 15 in.
   h = 12 in.

8. b = 6.5 yd.
   h = 42 yd.

9. b = 11 cm.
   h = 14 cm.

10. b = 27 km.
    h = 18 km.

11. Write two formulas that can be used to find the area of a rectangle.

Area

Triangles

A **triangle** is a three sided polygon.

The area (A) of a triangle equals $\frac{1}{2}$ the base (b) times the height (h).

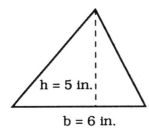

h = 5 in.

b = 6 in.

$A = \frac{1}{2} \mathbf{b\ x\ h}$

$A = \frac{1}{2}$ x 6 in. x 5 in.

$A = \frac{1}{2}$ x 30 in.

$A = 15\ \text{in.}^2$

Area, Triangles, Exercise 1. Use the formula to find the area of these triangles.

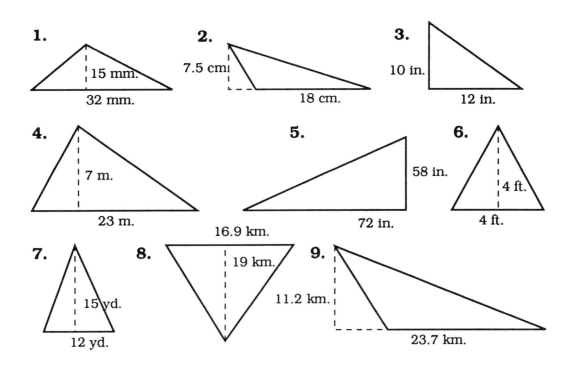

1.

15 mm.

32 mm.

2.

7.5 cm

18 cm.

3.

10 in.

12 in.

4.

7 m.

23 m.

5.

16.9 km.

6.

58 in.

72 in.

4 ft.

4 ft.

7.

15 yd.

12 yd.

8.

19 km.

9.

11.2 km.

23.7 km.

10. b = 13.7 m.
    h = 24 m.

12. b = 20 ft.
    h = $\frac{1}{2}$ ft.

14. b = 32.8 in.
    h = 12 in.

11. b = 57 yd.
    h = 12 yd.

13. b = 12 cm.
    h = 17 cm.

15. b = 30 km.
    h = 30 km.

Area, Triangles, Exercise 2. Use your knowledge to find the area of these figures.

1.

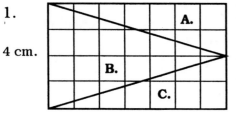

4 cm.

7 cm.

The area of:
△ A =
△ B =
△ C =
Total area =

2.

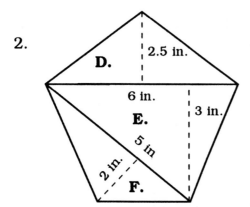

2.5 in.

6 in.

3 in.

5 in

2 in.

The area of:
△ D =
△ E =
△ F =
Total area =

3.

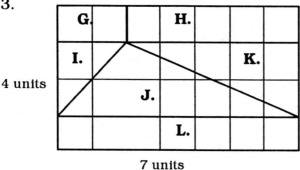

4 units

7 units

The area of:
▭ G =
▭ H =
△ I =
△ J =
△ K =
▭ L =
Total area =

4.

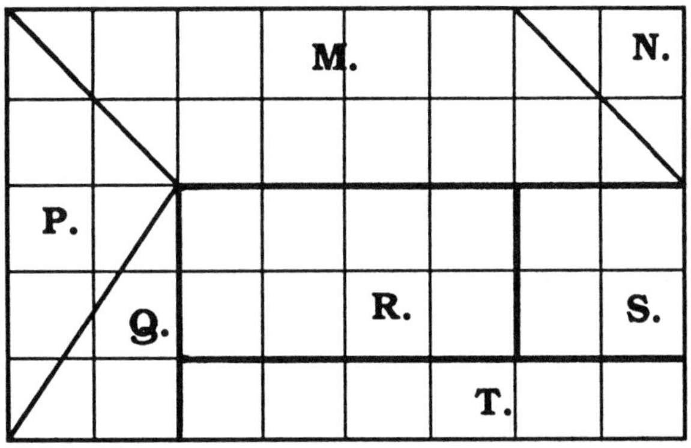

The area of:
▱ M =
△ N =
△ P =
△ Q =
▢ R =
▢ S =
▢ T =

Total area =

Area

Trapezoids

A **trapezoid** is a quadrilateral with only one pair of parallel sides.

The area (A) of a trapezoid is equal to $\frac{1}{2}$ height (h) times the sum of the bases (a + b).

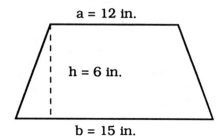

a = 12 in.

h = 6 in.

b = 15 in.

$A = \frac{1}{2} h (a + b)$

$A = \frac{1}{2} 6$ in. (12 in. + 15 in.)

$A = 3$ in. (12 in. + 15 in.)

$A = 81$ in.^{2}

Area, Trapezoids, Exercise 1. Find the area of these trapezoids.

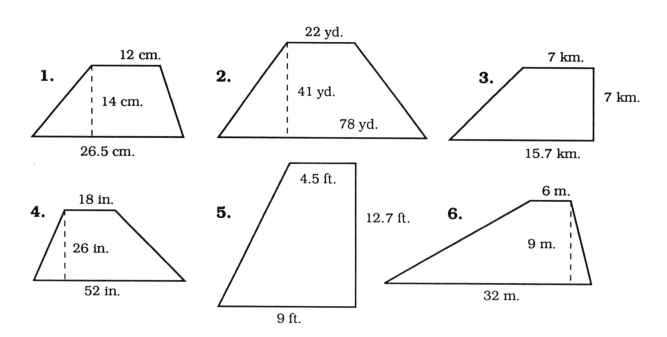

1. 12 cm. 14 cm. 26.5 cm.

2. 22 yd. 41 yd. 78 yd.

3. 7 km. 7 km. 15.7 km.

4. 18 in. 26 in. 52 in.

5. 4.5 ft. 12.7 ft. 9 ft.

6. 6 m. 9 m. 32 m.

Area, Trapezoids, Exercise 2. Use your knowledge of plane figures to find the area of each polygon. Be sharp, there are short cuts.

1.

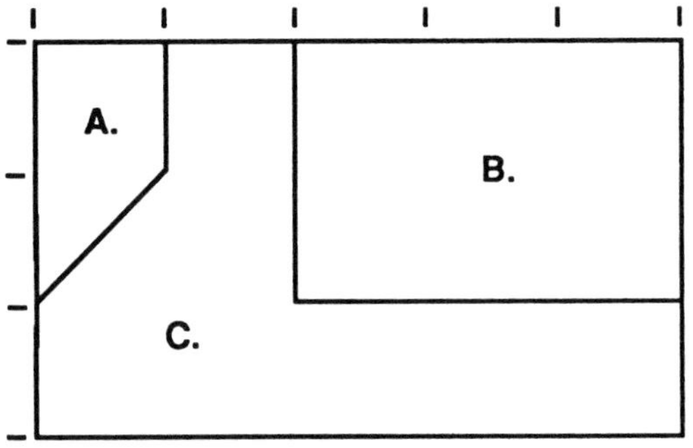

The figure is divided into equal units.

Area of:

Figure A =

Figure B =

Figure C =

Total area =

2.

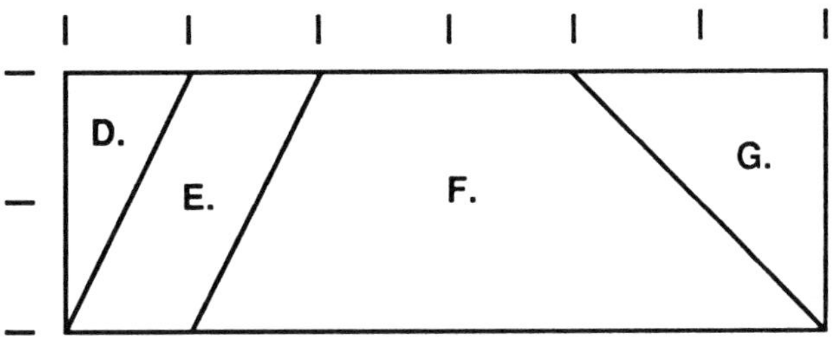

The figure is divided into equal units.

Area of:

△ D =

⧄ E =

◺ F =

△ G =

Total area =

hint: the area of the ⧄ can be found by subtraction.

Area

Circles

A **circle** is a plane geometric figure with all its points the same distance from its center.

Area (A) of a circle equals pi (π) times the radius (r) times the radius (r).

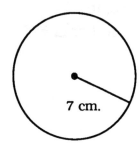

7 cm.

A = π r²
A = 3.14 x 7 cm. x 7 cm.
A = 3.14 x 49 cm.
A = 153.86 cm.

Circles, Exercise 1. Find the area of these circles.

1.

7 in.

2.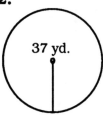

37 yd.

3.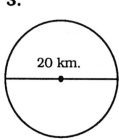

20 km.

4.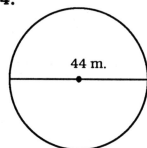

44 m.

5. radius = 15 yd.

6. radius = 8.5 m.

7. radius = 10.3 km.

8. diameter = 12 in.

9. diameter = 23 cm.

10. radius = 33 ft.

Circles, Exercise 2. Use your knowlege to solve these figures. Find the area.

1.

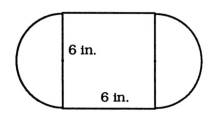

6 in.

6 in.

2.

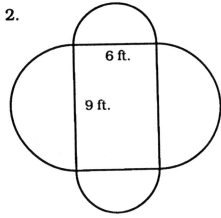

6 ft.

9 ft.

3.

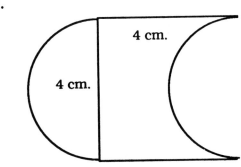

4 cm.

4 cm.

4.

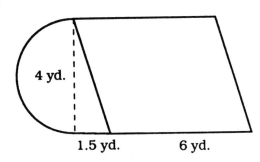

4 yd.

1.5 yd.   6 yd.

a. Solve the area by using 3 figures.

b. Solve the area by using 2 figures.

Polyhedrons

Polyhedrons are geometric figures which have multiple faces (sides) shaped like polygons. Polyhedrons are also three dimensional figures. They occupy space.

Here are two classes of polyhedrons with examples.

Polyhedrons: Prisms and Pyramids

Prisms have bases which are the same size and which are parallel.

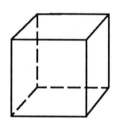 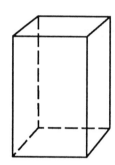 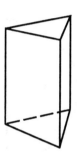

Cube or Square Prism   Rectangular Prism   Triangular Prism

Pyramids have one base with all triangular sides sharing the same vertex.

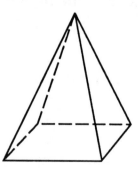 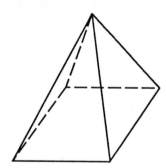 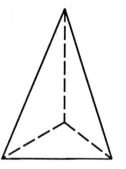

Square Pyramid   Rectangular Pyramid   Triangular Pyramid

Cones and cyclinders are not polyhedrons because their faces are not polygons. But cones and cylinders are three dimensional figures occupying space.

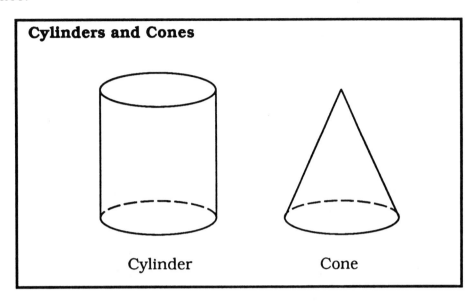

Cylinders and Cones

Cylinder   Cone

Polyhedron/Cones/Cylinders, Exercise 1. Write **yes** next to each figure that is a polyhedron. Write **no** next to each figure that is not a polyhedron.

1.

2.

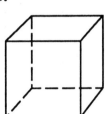

3.

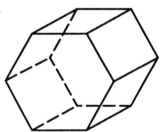

4.

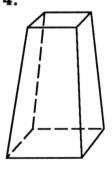

5.

6.

7.

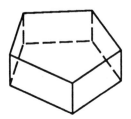

8.

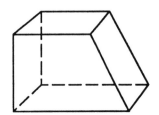

Polyhedrons
Surface Area

The surface area of a polyhedron can be detemined by finding the area of each face. For example, here is a simple rectangular prism.

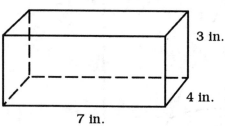

Front face =	7 in. x 3 in. = 21 sq. in.	(A = l w)
Top face =	7 in. x 4 in. = 28 sq. in.	(A = l w)
Back face =	7 in. x 3 in. = 21 sq. in.	(A = l w)
Bottom face =	7 in. x 4 in. = 28 sq. in.	(A = l w)
Right side face =	4 in. x 3 in. = 12 sq. in.	(A = l w)
Left side face =	4 in. x 3 in. = 12 sq. in.	(A = l w)
Total Surface Area = 122 in².		

Other polyhedrons, such as a square pyramid, are done similarly. Merely break the figure down into geometric shapes: 1 square, 4 equal triangles.

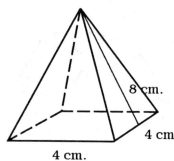

Bottom square face = 4 cm. x 4 cm.= 16 cm². $(A = s^2)$

Left face triangle = $\frac{1}{2}$ x 4 cm. x 8 cm. = 16 cm². $(A = \frac{1}{2} bh)$

Right face triangle = $\frac{1}{2}$ x 4 cm. x 8 cm. = 16 cm².

Back face triangle = $\frac{1}{2}$ x 4 cm. x 8 cm. = 16 cm².

Front face triangle = $\frac{1}{2}$ x 4 cm. x 8 cm. = 16 cm².

Total Surface Area = 80 cm².

Polyhedrons, Surface Area, Exercise 2. Find the surface area of these polyhedrons.

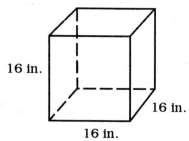

10 ft.   Triangular (isosceles) Prism

1. Bottom face (A = s²) =
   Top face =
   Left face =
   Right face =
   Front face =
   Back face =
   Total Surface Area =

2. Front △ face (A = $\frac{1}{2}$ bh) =
   Back △ face =
   Bottom ☐ face (A = lw) =
   Right side ☐ face =
   Left side ☐ face =
   Total Surface Area =

Polyhedrons, Surface Area, Exercise 3. Find the surface area of these polyhedrons.

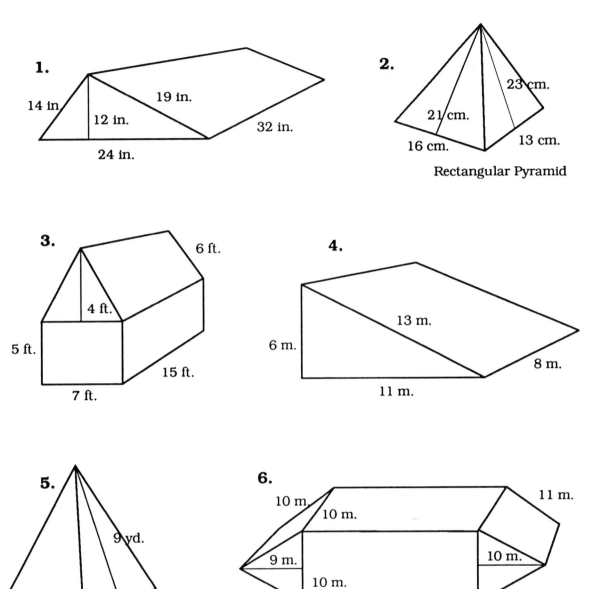

1.

14 in. 19 in. 12 in. 32 in. 24 in.

2.

23 cm. 21 cm. 16 cm. 13 cm.

Rectangular Pyramid

3.

6 ft. 4 ft. 5 ft. 15 ft. 7 ft.

4.

13 m. 6 m. 8 m. 11 m.

5.

9 yd. 7 yd. 7 yd.

Square Pyramid

6.

10 m 10 m. 11 m. 9 m. 10 m. 10 m. 25.5 m.

Volume is the inside space of a three dimensional figure. Volume is measured in cubic units -e.g., in.³ , or cu. in; cm.³ , or cu. cm.

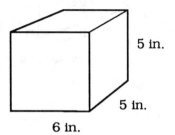

5 in.

5 in.

6 in.

The volume (V) of a prism is length (l) of base times width (w) of base times height (h).

V = l w h
V = 5 in. x 5 in. x 6 in.
V = 150 cu. in.

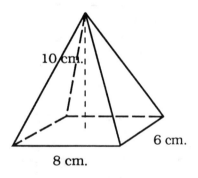

10 cm.

6 cm.

8 cm.

The volume of a pyramid is $\frac{1}{3}$ times the area of the base (b) times the height (h).

The height of a pyramid is a perpendicular height. The perpendicular height is from the top of the pyramid down to the base. The perpendicular makes a 90° angle with the base (represented by the dotted line labeled 10 cm.).

V = $\frac{1}{3}$ b h
V = $\frac{1}{3}$ x l x w x h
V = $\frac{1}{3}$ x 8 x 6 x 10
V = 160 cu. cm.

Polyhedrons, Volume, Exercise 4. Find the volume of each figure.

1.

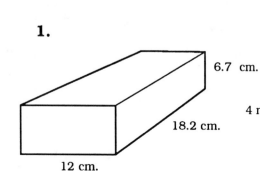

6.7 cm.

18.2 cm.

12 cm.

2.

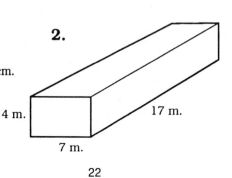

4 m.

17 m.

7 m.

3.

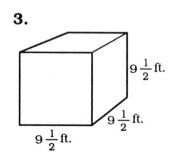

$9\frac{1}{2}$ ft.

$9\frac{1}{2}$ ft.

$9\frac{1}{2}$ ft.

4.

82 m.

40 m.

35 m.

5.

52 in.

42 in.

16 in.

6.

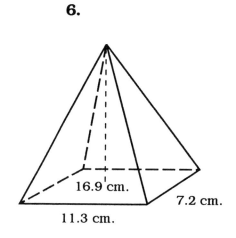

16.9 cm.

7.2 cm.

11.3 cm.

Polyhedrons, Volume, Exercise 5. Find the volume.

Rectangular Prisms

1. l = 14.7 in. **2.** l = 23 yd.   **3.** l = 142 ft.   **4.** l = 32 m.
w = 10.2 in.   w = 23.5 yd   w = 72 ft.   w = 74.7 m.
h = 12.4 in.   h = 24 yd.   h = 3 ft.   h = 24.5 m.

Pyramids with Rectangular Bases

5. l = $30\frac{1}{2}$ cm. **6.** l = 102 in.   **7.** l = 20 ft
w = 15 cm.   w = 105 in.   w = 30 ft.
h = 32 cm.   h = 92 in.   h = 120.1 ft.

8. How many cubic feet of cement must be used to pave a driveway 47.5 ft. long, 12 ft. wide, 4 inches deep?

9. How much storage space is in a container measuring 4.5 meters long, 2.7 meters wide, and 1.8 meters high?

10. How many cubic feet of earth must be dug to create a basement for a 57 foot by 30 foot house. The basement must have a floor 7 feet below ground.

23

Final Assessment Test

1. Perimeter-Circumference. Match the geometric shape with the the formula.

___ 1. $P = s + s + ... + s$ a. area of a rectangle
___ 2. $V = \frac{1}{3} bh$ b. circumference of a circle
___ 3. $A = \pi r^2$ c. volume of a pyramid
___ 4. $A = l\,w$ d. perimeter of a polygon
___ 5. $C = \pi d$ e. area of a triangle
___ 6. $P = 4s$ f. area of a circle
___ 7. $A = \frac{1}{2} h(a+b)$ g. perimeter of a rectangle
___ 8. $V = l\,w\,h$ h. area of a parallelogram
___ 9. $A = b\,h$ i. volume of a prism
___ 10. $P = 2\,(l + w)$ j. perimeter of a square
___ 11. $A = \frac{1}{2} b\,h$ k. area of a trapezoid

2. Find the perimeter or circumference.

a.   **b.**   **c.**   **d.**

9 cm.

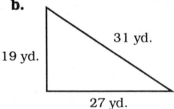

31 yd.
19 yd.
27 yd.

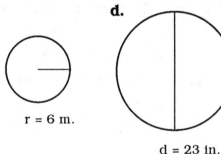

r = 6 m.

d = 23 in.

3. Find the area.

a.   **b.**   **c.**

$12\frac{1}{4}$ in.

$7\frac{1}{2}$ in.

14.9 mm.

11.2 km.

23.7 km.

d.   **e.**   **f.**

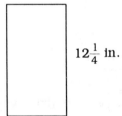

16.9 km.
19 km.

15.2 cm.

5.4 cm.

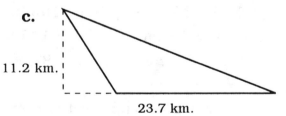

6 m.
9 m.
32 m.

24

3. Find the area of each figure.

a.

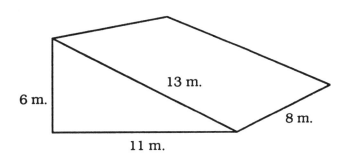

12 in.

12 in.

b.

4.5 m.

2 m.

4 m.

2 m.

4. Find the surface area of this figure.

13 m.

6 m.

8 m.

11 m.

5. Find the volume of these figures.

a.

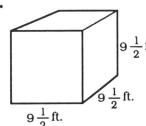

$9\frac{1}{2}$ ft.

$9\frac{1}{2}$ ft.

$9\frac{1}{2}$ ft.

b.

10 cm.

6 cm.

8 cm.

ANSWERS

Beginning Assessment Test. Page 1.

1. Perimeter-Circumference. Match the geometric shape with the the formula.

_d_	1. $P = s + s + \ldots + s$	a. area of a rectangle
_c_	2. $V = \frac{1}{3} bh$	b. circumference of a circle
_f_	3. $A = \pi r^2$	c. volume of a pyramid
_a_	4. $A = l\,w$	d. perimeter of a polygon
_b_	5. $C = \pi d$	e. area of a triangle
_j_	6. $P = 4s$	f. area of a circle
_k_	7. $A = \frac{1}{2} h(a+b)$	g. perimeter of a rectangle
_i_	8. $V = l\,w\,h$	h. area of a parallelogram
_h_	9. $A = b\,h$	i. volume of a prism
_g_	10. $P = 2\,(l + w)$	j. perimeter of a square
_e_	11. $A = \frac{1}{2}\,b\,h$	k. area of a trapezoid

2. Find the perimeter or circumference of these figures.

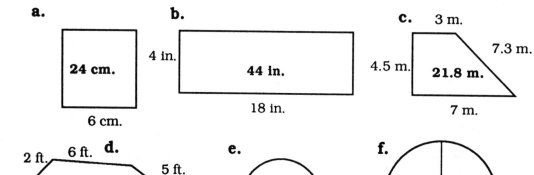

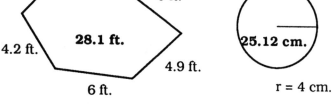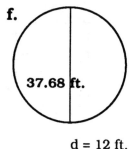

3. Find the area of all the figures above except *d* .

a. 36 cm.²   b. 72 in.²   c. 22.5 m.²   e. 50.24 cm.²   f. 113.04 ft²

26

4. Find the area of each figures.

a.

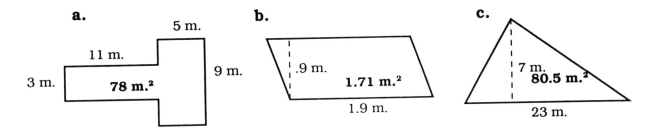

5 m.

11 m.

3 m. **78 m.²** 9 m.

b.

.9 m.

1.71 m.²

1.9 m.

c.

7 m.

80.5 m.²

23 m.

5. Find the surface area of this figure.

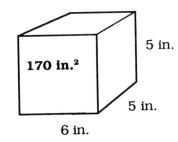

5 in.

170 in.²

5 in.

6 in.

6. Find the volume of each figure.

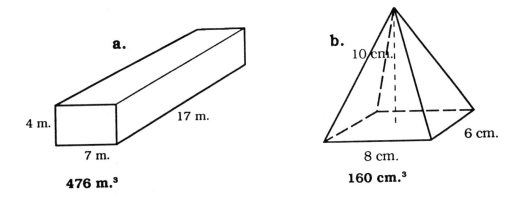

a.

4 m. 17 m.

7 m.

476 m.³

b.

10 cm.

6 cm.

8 cm.

160 cm.³

Perimeter, Squares/Rectangles, Exercise 1. Page 4.
   1. 80 cm.
   2. 82 m.
   3. 48 ft.
   4. 9.8 km.
   5. 122 m.
   6. 56 in.
   7. 42 ft.

Perimeter, Exercise 2. Page 4.
   1. 30 cm.
   2. 64 in.
   3. 41.5 m
   4. 77 yd.
   5. 108 in.
   6. 83.3 mm.
   7. 7 in. Hint: Determine the length of one unlabeled side.

Perimeter, Exercise 3. Page 4.
   1. 42.9 cm.
   2. 13 ft.
   3. equilateral triangle, 5 in.
   4. 27.5 m.
   5. 12 yd.

Circumference, Exercise 1. Page 6.
   1a. 18.84 cm.
   1b. 31.4 m.
   1c. 10.99 km.
   1d. 43.96 in.
   2a. 7.85 in.
   2b. 10.1736 yd.
   2c. 37.68 ft.
   2d. 10.2678 miles
   2e. 87.92 yd.
   3. c = π2r; or, c = 2πr

Area, Rectangles/Squares, Exercise 1. Page 8.
   1. 12.25 cm.²
   2. 24 km.²
   3. 2.8 in.²
   4. $91\frac{7}{8}$ in. ²
   5. 222.01 mm.²
   6. 768 m.²
   7. 289 ft.²
   8. $19\frac{15}{16}$ km.²
   9. 175,040 ft.²

Area, Rectangles/Squares, Exercise 2. Page 8.
   1. 161 tiles
   2. 2604 in.²
   3. 4 qts.
   4. 6000 yd.²
   5. 14 cm.
   6. 10.5 in.

Area, Rectangles/Squares, Exercise 3. Page 9.

      1. 78 m.^{2}

      2. 66 km.^{2}

      3. 85 yd.^{2}

      4. $1844\frac{4}{9}$ yd.^{2}

Area, Parallelograms, Exercise 1. Page 10.

      1. 144 km.^{2}

      2. 82.08 cm.^{2}

      3. 864 in.^{2}

      4. 1.71 m.^{2}

      5. 391 yd.^{2}

      6. 6724 mm.^{2}

      7. 180 in.^{2}

      8. 273 yd.^{2}

      9. 154 cm.^{2}

      10. 486 km.^{2}

      11. A = b x h or A = l x w

Area, Triangles, Exercise 1. Page 11.

1. 240 mm.^{2}	9. 132.72 km.^{2}
2. 67.5 cm.^{2}	10. 164.4 m.^{2}
3. 60 in.^{2}	11. 342 yd.^{2}
4. 80.5 m.^{2}	12. 5 ft.^{2}
5. 2088 in.^{2}	13. 102 cm.^{2}
6. 8 ft.^{2}	14. 196.8 in.^{2}
7. 90 yd.^{2}	15. 450 km.^{2}
8. 160.55 km.^{2}	

Area, Triangles, Exercise 2. Page 12.

1. △ A = 7 cm.^{2}
   △ B = 14 cm.^{2}
   △ C = 7 cm.^{2}
   Total Area = 28 cm.^{2}

2. △ D = 7.5 cm.^{2}
   △ E = 9 cm.^{2}
   △ F = 5 cm.^{2}
   Total Area = 21.5 cm.^{2}

3. ▢ G = 2 units^2
   ▢ H = 5 units^2
   △ I = 2 units^2
   △ J = 7 units^2
   △ K = 5 units^2
   ▢ L = 7 units^2
   Total Area = 28 units^2

4. ▱ M = 12 units^2
   △ N = 2 units^2
   △ P = 5 units^2
   △ Q = 3 units^2
   ▢ R = 8 units^2
   ▢ S = 4 units^2
   ▢ T = 6 units^2
   Total Area = 40 units^2

Area, Trapezoids, Exercise 1. Page 14.
1. 269.5 cm.²
2. 2050 yd.²
3. 79.45 km.²
4. 910 in.²
5. 85.725 ft.²
6. 171 m.²

Area, Trapezoids, Exercise 2. Page 15.
1. Figure A = 1.5 units²
Figure B = 6 units²
Figure C = 7.5 units²
Total Area = 15 units²
2. △ D = 1 unit²
▱ E = 2 units²
▱ F = 7 units²
△ G = 2 units²
Total Area = 12 units²

Circles, Exercise 1. Page 16

1. 158.86 in.²	5. 706.5 yd.²	9. 415.265 cm.²
2. 4298.66 yd.²	6. 226.865 m.²	10. 3419.46 ft.²
3. 314 km.²	7. 333.1226 km.²	
4. 1519.76 m.²	8. 113.04 in.²	

Circles, Exercise 2. Page 16
1. 64.26 in.²
2. 145.845 ft.²
3. 16 cm.²
4a. Semi-circle = 6.28 yd.²
Triangle = 3 yd.²
Parallelogram = 24 yd.²
Total Area = 33.28 yd.²
4b. Semi-circle = 6.28 yd.²
Trapezoid = 27 yd.²
Total Area = 33.28 yd.²

Polyhedrons, Exercise 1. Page 19.

1. no	5. no
2. yes	6. no
3. yes	7. yes
4. yes	8. yes

Polyhedrons, Surface Area, Exercise 2. Page 20.
1. Bottom face = 256 in.²
Top face = 256 in.²
Left face = 256 in.²
Right face = 256 in.²
Front face = 256 in.²
Back face = 256 in.²
Total Surface Area = 1536 in.²
2. Front triangle face = 60 ft.²
Back triangle face = 60 ft.²
Bottom rectangle face = 200 ft.²
Right rectangle face = 260 ft.²
Left rectangle face = 260 ft.²
Total Surface Area = 840 ft.²

Polyhedrons, Surface Area, Exercise 3. Page 21.

    1. 2112 in.²

        Hint: Front △ =   144 in.²

                 Back △ =   144 in.²

                 Bottom▭ =   768 in.²

                 Right ▭ =   608 in.²

                 Left ▭ =   448 in.²

    2. 843 cm.²

        Hint :   Front right △ =   149.5 cm.²

                 Front left   △ =   168 cm.²

                 Back right △ =   168 cm.²

                 Back left   △ =   149.5 cm.²

                 Bottom ▭ =   208 cm.²

    3. 533 ft.²

    4. 306 m.²

    5. 175 yd.²

    6. 1630 m.²

Polyhedrons, Volume, Exercise 4. Page 22.

    1. 1463.28 cm.³

    2. 476 m.³

    3. $857\frac{3}{8}$ ft.³

    4. 114,800 m.³

    5. 34,944 in.³

    6. 458.328 cm.³

Polyhedrons, Volume, Exercise 5. Page 23

    1. 1859.256 in.³

    2. 12,972 yd.³

    3. 30,672 ft.³

    4. 58,564.8 m.³

    5. 4880 cm.³

    6. 328,440 in.³

    7. 24,020 ft.³

    8. 190 ft.³

    9. 21.87 in.³

    10. 11,970 ft.³

Final Assessment Test. Page 24.

1. Perimeter-Circumference. Match the geometric shape with the the formula.

_d_   1. P = s + s +...+ s
_c_   2. V = $\frac{1}{3}$ bh
_f_   3. A= π r²
_a_   4. A = l w
_b_   5. C = π d
_j_   6. P = 4s
_k_   7. A = $\frac{1}{2}$ h(a+b)
_i_   8. V = l w h
_h_   9. A = b h
_g_   10. P = 2 (l + w)
_e_   11. A = $\frac{1}{2}$ b h

a. area of a rectangle
b. circumference of a circle
c. volume of a prism
d. perimeter of a polygon
e. area of a triangle
f. area of a circle
g. perimeter of a rectangle
h. area of a parallelogram
i. volume of a prism
j. perimeter of a square
k. area of a trapezoid

2. Find the perimeter or circumference.

a.
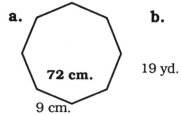
72 cm.
9 cm.

b.
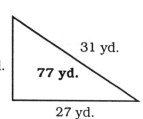
19 yd.   31 yd.
77 yd.
27 yd.

c.

37.68 m.
r = 6 m.

d.
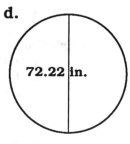
72.22 in.
d = 23 in.

3. Find the area.

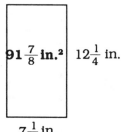
91$\frac{7}{8}$ in.²   12$\frac{1}{4}$ in.
7$\frac{1}{2}$ in.

222.01mm.²
14.9 mm.

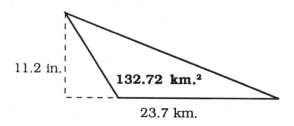
11.2 in.
132.72 km.²
23.7 km.

d.
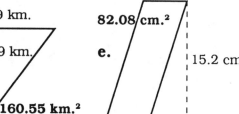
16.9 km.
19 km.
160.55 km.²

e.
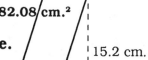
82.08 cm.²
15.2 cm.
5.4 cm.

f.
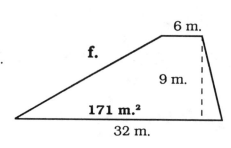
6 m.
9 m.
171 m.²
32 m.

3. Find the area of each figure.

a.

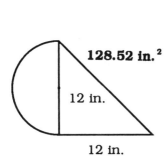

128.52 in.²

12 in.

12 in.

b.

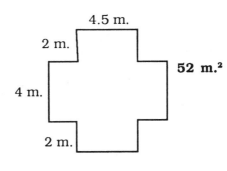

4.5 m.

2 m.

4 m.

52 m.²

2 m.

4. Find the surface area of this figure.

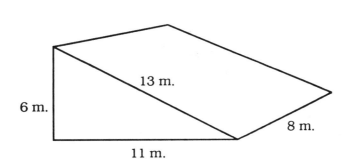

13 m.

6 m.

8 m.

11 m.

Top = 104 m.²
Bottom = 88 m. ²
Back = 48 m. ²
Side = 33 m. ²
Side = 33 m.²

Total = 306 m.²

5. Find the volume of these figures.

a.

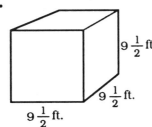

$9\frac{1}{2}$ ft.

$9\frac{1}{2}$ ft.

$9\frac{1}{2}$ ft.

$857\frac{3}{8}$ ft.³

b.

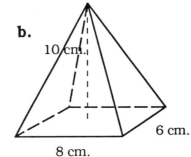

10 cm.

6 cm.

8 cm.

160 cm.³

English Series

The Straight Forward English Series

is designed to measure, teach, review, and master
specified English skills: capitalization and punctuation;
nouns and pronouns; verbs; adjectives and adverbs;
prepositions, conjunctions and interjections; sentences;
clauses and phrases, and mechanics.

Each workbook is a simple, straightforward approach to
learning English skills. Skills are keyed to major school
textbook adoptions.

Pages are reproducible.

GP-032	Capitalization and Punctuation
GP-033	Nouns and Pronouns
GP-034	Verbs
GP-035	Adjectives and Adverbs
GP-041	Sentences
GP-043	Prepositions, conjunctions, & Interjections

Advanced Series

Large editions

GP-055	Clauses & Phrases
GP-056	Mechanics
GP-075	Grammar & Diagramming Sentences

Discovering Literature Series

The Discovering Literature Series

is designed to develop an appreciation for literature and to improve
reading skills. Each guide in the series features an award winning
novel and explores a wide range of critical reading skills and
literature elements.

GP-076	A Teaching Guide to My Side of the Mountain
GP-077	A Teaching Guide to Where the Red Fern Grows
GP-078	A Teaching Guide to Mrs. Frisby & the Rats of NIMH
GP-079	A Teaching Guide to Island of the Blue Dolphins
GP-093	A Teaching Guide to the Outsiders
GP-094	A Teaching Guide to Roll of Thunder

Challenging Level

GP-090	The Hobbit: A Teaching Guide
GP-091	Redwall: A Teaching Guide
GP-092	The Odyssey: A Teaching Guide
GP-097	The Giver: A Teaching Guide
GP-096	Lord of the Flies: A Teaching Guide
GP-074	To Kill A Mockingbird: A Teaching Guide